636.7   Colson, Mary
COL   The truth about dogs:what dogs
         do when you're not looking

DATE DUE			
NOV 1 3 2017			
APR 0 8 2019			
MAY 0 2019			
JUN 0 1 2018			
FEB 0 2020			
SEP 1 2021			

PETS UNDERCOVER!

The TRUTH About DOGS

What Dogs Do When You're Not Looking

MARY COLSON

capstone

To contact Capstone Global Library please call 800-747-4992, or visit our web site
www.mycapstone.com

Edited by Helen Cox Cannons
Designed by Philippa Jenkins
Picture research by Morgan Walters
Production by Laura Manthe
Originated by Capstone Global Library Ltd
Printed and bound in Canada
10038S17

Library of Congress Cataloging-in-Publication Data
Cataloging-in-publication information is on file with the Library of Congress.
Written by Mary Colson.
ISBN 978-1-4109-8606-1 (library binding)
ISBN 978-1-4109-8618-4 (eBook PDF)

Acknowledgments
We would like to thank the following for permission to reproduce photographs: All
photographs by Capstone Studio: Karon Dubke.

We would like to thank Caroline Kisko, Secretary and Communications Director at the Kennel
Club for her invaluable help in the preparation of this book.

Every effort has been made to contact copyright holders of any material reproduced in this
book. Any omissions will be rectified in subsequent printings if notice is given to the publisher.

All the Internet addresses (URLs) given in this book were valid at the time of going to press.
However, due to the dynamic nature of the Internet, some addresses may have changed, or
sites may have changed or ceased to exist since publication. While the author and publisher
regret any inconvenience this may cause readers, no responsibility for any such changes can be
accepted by either the author or the publisher.

Some words are shown in bold, **like this**. You can find
out what they mean by looking in the glossary.

TABLE OF CONTENTS

Hello!

Woof, woof! That's dog talk for "Hello!" I'm so excited to meet you! I'm Ted, and I'm going to tell you all about myself. You will learn about the crazy things I do when my owners aren't at home! I may look soft, cuddly, and cute but deep down I'm pretty wild!

I'm Your Best Friend

Matt, Beth, Mom, and I make a great team. We're best friends, and we look after each other. I'm very **loyal**.

When they get up, everyone comes and pats me to say "Hi!" Before they go to work and school, they give me fresh water, my dry food, and some meat. I get some dog treats too, if I'm lucky. Yum!

I'm a Top Explorer!

Bye, see you later!

When Mom and the kids leave, I wander around the house. I like to explore. I'm very smart and learn quickly. I can open the doors by jumping up and twisting the handles. I like to sniff around in cupboards too. Let's see how messy Beth's bedroom is today...

Super Sniffers

If I may say so myself, I have an amazing nose! I'm much better at smelling than you are. My nose has millions of **scent glands**. I can sniff out danger as well as friends and treats.

I have great whiskers too! They help me find my way in the dark.

Ooh! What's that under the couch? Crunchy!

Listen Up!

Woof! What's that outside?

Dogs have much better hearing than humans do. I can sometimes hear things from more than 1 mile (1.6 kilometers) away. I can even tell when the family are on your way home before they arrive. I sometimes lean my head to the side to hear better.

Warning Bells

Grooooowl! I can hear another dog! Why is he in my **territory**? The nerve! Woof! Woof! There, I think I scared him off.

I use lots of different noises to show my feelings. I **yelp** if I'm hurt and **whimper** if I'm sick. When I'm really upset, I growl.

Don't Scare Me!

Just like you, I don't like being scared. I react to defend myself, my family, and my **territory**. I bark loudly or **whine**. If I can see danger, my eyes narrow. I'm ready to attack. My ears go up, and so does my tail. That's my **signal** for "stay away!"

A Very Quick Clean

Slurp! That's better! I like to clean bits of food from around my mouth and dirt from my paws. That's about it for my washing **routine**!

Matt and Beth think I smell stinky sometimes, but I like my smell. But it is fun when they give me a bath. Afterwards, Mom uses her hairdryer on me, and I feel like a doggy model!

Chewing Machine

Look what Beth has left under the sofa—her slipper!

I love to chew on things. I like **gnawing** on **rawhide**. Rawhide helps to keep my jaws and teeth strong. Usually, I prefer to chew real food but, until feeding time, Beth's slipper will do!

Playing is Practicing

Just like you, I love to play. Playing keeps me fit and strong. I like playing with my toys. The best ones make a noise. I like squeaky toys because it's like hunting. I pretend I'm chasing my **prey**. This also helps me practice keeping my home safe.

Sometimes I bark when I play to show that I'm having fun.

Walks!

Woof! Woof! Mom, Beth, and Matt are home! Great! Now I can go for my walk. I hope we go to the park. I can run around the park when they let me off the leash. They throw balls, and I race to catch them. If I do a really good catch, I get a tasty treat!

When You Go to Sleep...

Yawn! I get sleepy in the evenings. When Mom, Matt, and Beth go to bed, they always say "Goodnight. Don't wake us up!"

I settle down in my bed. I don't go straight to sleep though. I am watching and listening...

What's that noise? There it is again. Right, I'm ready. Woof! Woof! Woof!

How Wild is *Your* Dog?

1. What does your dog do when it hears a noise outside?

a) It growls for a minute then just ignores it.

b) It runs and hides behind the sofa.

c) It barks like crazy.

2. What does your dog do with noisy toys?

a) It pushes them away.

b) It whines because it doesn't like the noise.

c) It bites them with its sharp teeth and won't let go.

3. What does your dog do when you leave your shoes out?

a) It picks them up and carries them to your room.

b) It sniffs them then curls up with them in its basket.

c) It chews, bites, and gnaws them to shreds!

4. What does your dog do when you let it off the lead?

a) It sniffs the ground and eats some grass.

b) It stays close to you for safety.

c) It races off, happy to be running.

To find out how wild your dog is, check the results on page 32.

Glossary

gnaw (NAW)—to keep biting on something

loyal (LOI-uhl)—being true to someone or something

prey (PRAY)—animal hunted and eaten by another animal

rawhide (RAW-hyde)—the skin of cattle or other animals before it has been soaked in a special solution and made into leather

routine (roo-TEEN)—a regular way or pattern of doing tasks

scent gland (SENT GLAND)—a special organ in the body that create smells

signal (SUG-nuhl)—action which gives some information or a message

territory (TER-uh-tor-ee)—an area of land that an animal claims as its own to live in

whimper (WIM-pur)—to make weak, crying noises

whine (WINE)—to complain or moan about something in an annoying way

yelp (YELP)—to cry out in pain

Find Out More

Books

Ganeri, Anita. *Ruff's Guide to Caring for Your Dog.* Pets' Guides. Chicago: Heinemann, 2013.

Guillain, Charlotte. *Dogs.* Animal Abilities. Chicago: Raintree, 2013.

Rustad, Martha E.H. *Dogs.* Little Scientist. North Mankato, Minn.: Capstone, 2015.

Internet Sites

FactHound offers a safe, fun way to find Internet sites related to this book. All of the sites on FactHound have been researched by our staff.

Here's all you do:

Visit *www.facthound.com*

Type in this code: 9781410986061

Check out projects, games and lots more at **www.capstonekids.com**

Index

Quiz Answers:

Mostly As: Your dog is very chill! He's not bothered by anything. He's happy to do his own thing in a very calm way.

Mostly Bs: Your dog likes the quiet life. He would rather hide than face up to danger. He's supposed to protect you, not the other way around!

Mostly Cs: You clearly have the wildest dog in town! He'll take on anyone and anything!